JOSEPH AND HIS BROTHERS

Long ago, a good man called Jacob

lived in the land of Canaan. 's

many sons looked after the and

 . To his favourite son, ,

he gave a fine of many colours.

This made the other brothers jealous.

They also hated because of

his dreams, which showed him ruling

over the family.

One day, sent  to see

if his brothers were safe guarding the

 and in the wilderness.

The brothers saw coming in

his  of many colours. "Let us

kill him," they said. But Reuben asked

them not to shed 's blood, so

they put him in a and left him

to die. Reuben planned secretly to

rescue later.

The other brothers were resting at

an near the when a

 came by. Judah said, "Let us

sell to these traders." The

others agreed, so was taken

from the and led away in the

 to be a slave in Egypt.

Then the brothers killed a ,

put its blood on the  of many

colours and took it back to ,

saying wild animals had killed .

 was full of grief.

In Egypt, became the slave of , captain of 's  . was very pleased with 's work and made him the head of his servants. 's wife fell in love with and wanted him for herself, but rejected her. So 's wife told lies to her husband,

saying that  had insulted her,

and  put  in prison.

In prison, was able to explain the meaning of dreams to two of 's servants. Later, when himself had strange dreams, he asked to explain them.

 told , "I saw seven thin eating up seven fat , and seven thin ears of  eating up seven fat ears of  ."

ordered to explain these dreams.

explained that seven years of good would be followed by seven years of bad .

"What can I do?" asked .

 replied, "Put a wise man in charge of the so that enough is stored in the good years to feed everyone in the years of bad ."

Then said, "I see that God is with you," and he commanded to take charge of Egypt's .

 was pleased with and

gave him  and gold .

For seven years, stored the

 , so that the people would have

food when the was bad.

Then, during the bad s,

 's brothers came to Egypt to

buy food. knew them at once,

but they did not recognise .

"Why are you here?" he asked them.

"We have come to buy food from you because our has failed," answered the brothers. But pretended not to believe them.

"You are spies," he said, and he told his  to put them in prison.

After three days the  let them out.  sent them back to their father, , except for Simeon.

"Return with your brother, ,"

said , "or I will have Simeon

put to death."

was unwilling for his youngest son, , to go to Egypt.

"I have already lost ," cried , "I cannot now lose ."

But the people needed food, so in the end had to send back with his brothers. was in tears when he saw come in.

released Simeon and sold his brothers all the food they needed. As their was about to depart, told the  to hide his silver inside 's .

When they had left, said to his , "Find my silver ." They rode after the brothers and the was found in 's .

"Put him to death," said .

"No!" said Judah. "Put us to death instead."

Then knew that his brothers were no longer bad. He could not pretend any more and told his brothers who he really was. They were amazed.

"Go back to ," said , "and bring him and all his family, and  and , back here to live with me in Egypt."